★ REFLECTIONS OF A ★
BLACK COWBOY

BOOK ONE ★ COWBOYS

★ REFLECTIONS OF A ★
BLACK COWBOY

BY ROBERT H. MILLER

ILLUSTRATED BY RICHARD LEONARD

SILVER BURDETT PRESS

Published by Silver Burdett Press, Inc., a division of Simon & Schuster, Inc.,
Prentice Hall Bldg., Englewood Cliffs, NJ 07632.
Designed by Leslie Bauman
Manufactured in the United States of America
10 9 8 7 6 5 4 3 2 1

Library of Congress Cataloging-in-Publication Data

Miller, Robert H. (Robert Henry)
Reflections of a Black cowboy / by Robert H. Miller.
p.   cm. — (America in the modern world)
Summary: Examines the contributions Black cowboys have made to this country
and to the legacy of the West, focusing on the lives of Dead Wood Dick,
Cherokee Bill, Willie Kennard, Mary Fields, and Bill Pickett.
Includes bibliographical references (p. 79)
Contents: bk. 1. Cowboys.
1. Afro-American cowboys—West (U.S.)—Biography—Juvenile literature.   2.
West (U.S.)—Biography—Juvenile literature.   3. West (U.S.)—Social life and
customs—Juvenile literature. [1. Cowboys. 2. Afro-Americans—Biography.
3. West (U.S.)—Biography.]   I. Title.   II. Series: America in the modern
world (Unnumbered)
F596.M646   1990
978′ .00496073022—dc20
[B]   90-8661
[920]   CIP
ISBN 0-382-24079-0 (lib. bdg.) ISBN 0-382-24084-7 (pbk.)   AC

DEDICATION

To all five thousand or more black cowboys who drove cattle through the Chisholm, Western, and Goodnight-Loving trails. To you who braved freezing rain, dust storms, swollen rivers, buffalo stampedes, cattle rustlers, sickness, bad food, and through it all, worked so hard. Only you could have done it. This book reflects on you and the mighty contributions you made to this country and to the legacy of the Old West.

CONTENTS

PREFACE

Welcome to *Reflections of a Black Cowboy*. The books in this series were written to introduce you, the reader, to African-American people who helped settle the West. You'll meet cowboys, pioneers, soldiers, scouts, and mail drivers, and be part of history as our narrator the Old Cowboy remembers some stories from days gone by.

As young boys, my brother John and I would sit on the floor around my mother's favorite chair, waiting quietly for her to read us a story. She liked to read to us about faraway places and magical times. When I closed my eyes, I could see myself in the story—as a bystander or one of the main characters or often as the hero.

Like many black children growing up in the fifties, my heroes were drawn from the movies. Many of my favorite movies were westerns. Judging from what I saw in these movies, I figured there were no black cowboys. In the movies, most blacks had roles in the background as cooks or shoeshine boys or stable hands. Unfortunately, those weren't exactly the roles I had in mind for myself when I strapped on my play gun and holster outfit.

It was after one of those games of Cowboys and Indians that my mother told John and me a few new stories about her uncles, Ed and Joe Cloud. We thought "Cloud" was a strange-sounding name. Our mother explained that our great uncles were cowboys who had traveled throughout Texas and Mexico. Often, they had to shoot their way out of trouble on cattle drives.

From that day on, John and I had a different perspective when we played our games of Cowboys and Indians. Instead of Hollywood movie stars, our uncles became our heroes.

This book is an effort to help define our cultural heritage and to pay tribute to Ed and Joe Cloud and all the other black men and women who helped tame the West.

Journey back with me now to that place called the wild wild West, where you can be whoever *you* want. All you need is a fast horse, some boots, and a saddle. Now close your eyes—enjoy the ride!

Robert Miller

INTRODUCTION

As long as people have been raising cattle, there have been cowboys. When we look up the definition of "cowboy," we see that it describes a person "... who herds cattle." This description can be traced all the way back to ancient Egypt. Cattle have been around for a very long time, and there has always been someone to herd and breed them. However, never has the word "cowboy" taken on such mythic proportions as it has in America. In the American West, being a cowboy was more than just a profession. It spawned a whole way of life.

When America was in its infancy, the American Indians were our first cattle herders. They scouted and captured herds of wild horses, then "broke" them so they could be ridden. They also knew how to herd cattle without having to fence them in, as European ranchers did, to show ownership. The Indians took only what they needed; they were never greedy to possess the land or herds.

After the Civil War, Americans turned their attention westward. It was a time for expansion, a time for the country to patch up the differences between the North and South and look toward a common future. The West was a perfect place to begin. Wild Texas longhorn steers roamed the Great Plains in abundance after the Civil War. Because most Texans had gone off to war, these cows had been left to run free and multiply. Now that there was a demand again for beef in the North and East, Texans saw a market for their skills and the natural resources of their land.

Texas ranchers were willing and able to serve up as much beef as the North and East could eat, but they had to overcome one major problem—manpower. Where would they find men strong, skilled, and brave enough to take longhorn steers across thousands of miles of dangerous territory and get them to markets on time? These men would have to fight off outlaws and contend with rain storms, buffalo stampedes, swollen rivers, hail and dust, Indian raids, cold lonely nights in uncharted regions, as well as attacks on their herds by mountain lions, wolves, and coyotes. The men also had to be trustworthy, since they were counted on to bring the herds in on time with as little loss of livestock as possible.

African Americans were eager after the Civil War to take their place as American citizens. In the West, they found themselves in the right place with the right skills to gain immediate employment. Slavery, despite its wickedness, had produced a new breed of cowboy who seemed perfectly matched to the needs of the Texas ranchers. While working on plantations, slaves fine-tuned the art of herding, roping, and branding cows and horses. But African Americans possessed a legacy of these skills that went much further back than the days of slavery. In Africa, the ancestors of these slaves bred horses, domesticated cows, goats, sheep, dogs, and cats long before the Europeans discovered the place they eventually named America. African religion stressed a common link between man, his environment, and the universe that gave African Americans a natural ease in dealing with animals and nature. Europeans did not understand these religions and forbade Africans to practice them once they arrived in America. Nonetheless, the skills that these African Americans possessed with horses and cattle was passed down from one generation to the next and came in handy as the West was opened up for settlement.

Texas ranchers didn't have time to train cowboys after the war. The state was in a terrible economic mess, and the ranchers had to rush their cattle onto the new trails to stay in business. Because of this, a person who wanted to be a cowboy had to come to the range with the skills and savvy to succeed on the long trail north. Freed slaves and black ex-soldiers from the Civil War could smell the opportunity and sense of freedom in Texas, and when they arrived the white ranchers hired them right away. The need for experienced men to herd cattle to Kansas and Nebraska was greater than the supply, so the new men saddled up. This was a historic moment for black men and women in America. The word "cowboy" took on a new meaning.

When history books today write about the Old West— about how cowboys saved wagon trains full of white settlers and drove cattle up the Chisholm Trail—rarely are these men referred to as African Americans. Yet, of the more than thirty-eight thousand cowboys that drove cattle during the heyday of the West, one out of every four was African American. That's more than eight thousand men.

Reflections of a Black Cowboy was written to enlighten today's young reader. If we, as a culturally-mixed nation, are going to understand each other, then the truth about America's history must be told. Each racial and ethnic group has contributed its talent, energy, and lives to build what we know as America. No one group can lay claim to this great land because it belongs to no one. All we can do is to manage it in the best and most productive way possible.

These stories about Nat Love, ''Cherokee Bill,'' Mary Fields, Bill Pickett, and Willie Kennard place the splendor of the West in a larger cultural arena. As the West was settled and built, the exploits of these individuals became legends, and great stories about them were passed around many a campfire. Over time though, these legends have been forgotten. Now is the moment to remember again the contributions of these brave and colorful African Americans.

Although these stories have been somewhat embellished to make them entertaining, the people and events mentioned in them are all real. Cherokee Bill did lead a rather dramatic life, but he also learned that crime does not pay. Willie Kennard was a real African-American man who transformed the lawless mining town of Yankee Hill, Colorado, into a safe place for women and children. Nat Love was truly an American hero, right along with Bill Pickett and Mary Fields. I think you'll enjoy these stories, and I hope they make you ask more questions about what really happened during the development of the West and what significant roles other African Americans played.

Now find your favorite easy chair and get ready to go on a Western adventure with Sundown and the Old Cowboy.

HOW THE
OLD COWBOY
MET SUNDOWN

Once upon a time in Montana, in an old wooden shack on the outskirts of town, lived an Old Cowboy. At night, he rocked in his favorite chair and gazed into the heavens while he puffed on his old corncob pipe. Not far from his side was his best friend—his dog, Sundown.

The Old Cowboy had found Sundown hobbling along the road one evening. He knew, by the torn ear, that the dog had been in a fight, probably with a wolf or coyote. Carefully, the Old Cowboy moved toward Sundown.

"That's a boy. Just take it easy. I want to look at that ear," he said.

Sundown backed up slowly and growled, showing all his

teeth. The Old Cowboy stopped dead in his tracks. No animal had ever acted like that with him before. The Old Cowboy's senses, keenly sharpened by time, told him that something was very wrong.

When the wind shifted just a bit, the Old Cowboy's nose caught a familiar scent. Turning his head ever so slightly, he saw a mountain lion the size of a mule about to leap right at him.

"Looks like I got myself fixed up sideways," the Old Cowboy thought to himself. On one side of him, the lion, its tail swishing this way and that, eyed him from its hiding spot among the tall grass at the roadside. On the other, his growl growing meaner with every breath, Sundown slinked forward to meet the big cat.

Sundown's bravery came as a kind of signal to the Old Cowboy. It seemed as if that battered old mutt wanted to help him save his life.

With his back to the mountain lion, the Old Cowboy watched Sundown, his teeth bared and ready, take first one then another step toward the cat. The spunky dog looked as though it had the guts to rip out the heart of a buffalo.

"We're in on this roundup together, little fella," the Old Cowboy said under his breath. Then, quicker than light breaking through a dark room, he fell to the ground, and Sundown leaped over him and onto the back of the mountain lion, fighting for all he was worth.

The Old Cowboy had seen fights between wild stallions, and even fights between wolves and coyotes, but not in all his days had he seen a fight between a mongrel and a mountain lion.

Sundown and the mountain lion laid in to each other, tumbling head over heels in a dusty ball at the edge of the road. For a moment, the big cat shook Sundown and had him pinned under his front paws, and it looked as if the scrappy canine was going to be eaten alive. Somehow, Sundown slipped out of the mountain lion's grasp, and a second later he was riding the ferocious cat and biting clean through its ear. The cat howled in pain and tossed Sundown into the middle of the road. The two animals froze and sized one another up as they caught their breath before their final dust up. Sundown clinched a piece of ear victoriously in his mouth; the cat spat out a tuft of fur that had come from Sundown's front leg.

All the while, like a blind man searching for his cane, the Old Cowboy clawed the ground, looking desperately for his six-shooter. He knew, even though this brave mongrel dog was giving his best, that the mountain lion was too tough to be beaten.

Just as he found his pistol, the two creatures jumped at one another again, snapping and yelping as they chased each other in a figure eight in the middle of the road. Carefully aiming his revolver, the Old Cowboy squeezed the trigger, and as suddenly as the crack of gunfire, the mountain lion's fighting days ended.

Sundown hobbled over to the Old Cowboy. Laying down at the Old Cowboy's feet, the dog began to lick his wounds.

"You're one scrappy pup," the Old Cowboy said as he holstered his pistol and patted Sundown's back. "I reckon I owe you one. Now what do I call you?" the Old Cowboy asked. By then the sun was setting. The Old Cowboy snapped his fingers and said, "Sundown, that's your name. Sundown, let's go home."

It was only when they began to make their way home that they noticed the half moon which had come up over the distant hills. Sundown yipped at the moon, and the Old Cowboy smiled. They were both lucky to be alive, and from that day on the two of them were always together.

Sundown and the Old Cowboy got to be a well-known pair on the plains of Montana, and by and by other cowboys sought them out when they were looking for hospitality and a good story to make the night pass quicker. Always the Old Cowboy's first story would begin: "Did I ever tell you how I first hooked up with my partner Sundown . . ." Sundown would look up at the Old Cowboy and let out a satisfied yawn. No man and beast had ever needed each other more than those two.

One day, nobody knows when, the Old Cowboy and Sundown just disappeared. According to the legend, sometimes at night, not long after the sun goes down, you can hear the Old Cowboy call out to Sundown.

"Sundown, old partner, come over here and curl up for a spell. There's a story I want to tell you about someone I once knew." Then the Old Cowboy rubs his hands together as though to warm himself and launches into stories about his adventures as a black cowboy and about other black people he knew that helped settle the West.

If it's a clear night and the winds are blowing just right, listen carefully, and you might hear the Old Cowboy telling those stories to Sundown.

NAT LOVE, "DEADWOOD DICK"

Sundown, the West back in the old days was something to see. Settlers in covered wagons lined the plains like stars in a summer night sky. But there was one group of people who didn't like what they saw—the Indians. See, the Indians had lived on the land for many, many years. They had a special respect for nature and her creatures. In fact, the only animals they killed were those they needed to feed and clothe their families. Well, watching all these new arrivals come and make claims on their land was hard to take, and many fights broke out between the Indians and the white settlers. On the other hand, Indians and black people got along pretty well, maybe because they shared a common enemy. See, the white man was trying to take advantage of the Indians just like he did black people in the South. One black *man seeking a new future in the West wound up having quite an adventure in Indian territory.*

Nat Love left the South and followed his instincts West, like a bobcat returning to the wild, when he was still a young man. Nat was about fifteen when he arrived in Kansas, full of smoke and fire, with more courage than men twice his age.

From what I remember, Nat was born in 1854 on a plantation in Nashville, Tennessee. He learned the meaning of hard work at an early age, because Nat and his family were slaves on that plantation.

"I'll be the Yankee and you be the Rebel," said little Nat.

"No, you be the Rebel and I'll be the Yankee," his friend William said.

"It's my gun, I'll be the Yankee," Nat replied, as he snatched the stick away from William. "Bam, bam, I killed a Rebel," said Nat, pointing the stick at his friend.

Seven-year-old Nat was playing soldier because the Civil War had just started. He would gather all the boys on the plantation, and they would pretend a war was going on and they were fighting for their freedom. No slave wanted to fight for slavery, so the Rebels were the enemy. Since nobody wanted to be the enemy, Nat and his little gang went out into the countryside in search of one.

"Company, halt. Spread out, men," Nat yelled. "We got them surrounded." He and his men spread out. One group went west and the other east. "When I give the order, charge. Charge!"

All of Nat's soldiers charged right into a nest of bees. That day, they got more than they bargained for. Those bees put up a good fight and had Nat's men on the run, all the way home.

"Nat Love, where have you been, boy!" asked his mother, as he ran into his house all covered with welts. "I told you to stay out of Mister Thompson's honey farm. Now just look at you!"

"We surrounded the Rebels and charged, and we won," said Nat.

"You look like you won! Now go and bring me a jar of ointment," his mother replied.

When the Civil War was over, Nat and his family, along with all the other slaves, were set free. It was a joyous moment. All those years of working for nothing were over.

"Now we gets paid for our work," Nat's father declared. A proud man, Nat's father bought some land, and tried farming for a while. But his good health had been taken from him. Working all those backbreaking years on a plantation took its toll, and he died one evening while he was plowing his field. Nat's father left his wife and three children to fend for themselves.

Already fifteen, Nat was growing up fast. The feeling for adventure had started calling him. But after his father died, money was hard to come by, and he knew he had to put off leaving home and take over as head of the family. Nat was a natural leader, and his sister, brother, and mother relied on him.

The Love's farm didn't yield much in tobacco, and what little money they had went for rent. Nat knew you sure can't get blood from a turnip. Then Nat remembered that there was a horse ranch not far from where he lived. The owner had two sons about his age. So he went off to try his luck there.

"Hey, your pop around?" asked Nat.

One of the sons gave Nat the once over, and said, "No, he ain't here. Who wants to know?"

"The name is Nat Love. I live down the road a piece. I thought your father might need an extra hand around here."

By that time, the other brother came from around the barn. "Who's he?" he asked his brother. "Nobody. He's looking for work. We ain't hiring," said the first brother. The other brother whispered something in his brother's ear which made him smile.

"Follow me," the first one said.

Nat followed them to the back of the barn. There, in the corral, were some young colts their father had just bought. Now these two white boys figured to have some fun with young Nat.

"If you can ride any one of them, we'll give you ten cents," said one brother, grinning.

Ten cents was a lot of money in those days. Nat looked at the colts and thought about how much he needed the money. "I'll do it," he said.

That was the beginning of Nat Love's career. He climbed up on the fence, jumped on the back of that wild colt, and took off. Both boys were hollering and laughing, but Nat stayed on. That colt jumped and bucked all over the barnyard. Finally, tired out from all that bucking, the colt started trotting around the barnyard like he was used to carrying somebody. The brothers stopped laughing, congratulated Nat for such a great ride, and paid him his ten cents. Well, Nat broke three horses that day and collected thirty cents. He thought he was a rich man.

Nat went back to the ranch every Sunday after that, until he had enough money to buy his mother a sunbonnet and a pretty dress.

Nat's family worked hard and, with the money Nat was making breaking horses, things soon began to turn around for everyone. Tobacco made a profit at the market that year, and there was enough money left over to stock up on food for the winter.

"Mother, things look like they improving mighty fine around here now," said Nat. "What you think?"

"You don't have to play the fox with me, Nat Love," she replied. "I done seen that yonder look on your face for some time. I don't want you to go, but you right. Things is better now, thanks to God."

"You sure you gonna be all right?" asked Nat.

"I never seen much of the world, son. Maybe one day you come back and tell me what's on the other side of the mountain."

Nat hugged his mother, his sister, and his brother. Then he saddled his horse and headed West. The year was 1869 and Nat Love was fifteen.

All the years of hard work on the farm had made his young body strong and given him a spirit that even a wild mustang stallion couldn't match. Loaded down with confidence and charm, Nat rode into Dodge City, Kansas, like he owned it. He took to Dodge City like a thirsty man takes to water. It was a wild town full of adventure. Everywhere he looked, there were cowboys—sitting in silver saddles on big prancing horses, decked out in their best clothes and showing off to beat the band. Nat had never seen cowboys before now. When he took in all of this, he wanted to be a cowboy in the worst way.

Well, he started asking around about where to find work. "If you're looking for ranch work, sonny, go over to the Melody Saloon. That's where the cowboys always go to wet their whistles," said a stranger.

Nat had been watching how a cowboy carries himself so, by the time he walked into the saloon, he had a style about him. The place was full of cowboys from all over. Nat wasn't sure who to approach, but he decided to pick the meanest-looking cowboy he could find. That way, he figured, the others would see that he was serious. The bar seemed a likely place to start.

Nat approached this one tough-looking fellow. "Pardon me, stranger. Where can a man find work in these parts?"

The man stared at Nat like you would stare at a tree if it asked you for the time. Then he turned away without saying a word.

Nat figured this was some kind of test, so he tapped the man on his shoulder. "I said, where can a man find work around here?"

Conversation at the bar died down. The stranger turned to Nat. "Don't ever put your hands on me again, sonny, or I'll kill you," he said.

Cowboys in the bar stopped whatever they were doing. All eyes were on Nat. As stubborn as a mule, Nat wasn't about to show fear. He stepped back slowly, eyes steady on the stranger, and said, "I'm looking for work, mister, what're you looking for?"

After staring at young Nat for a minute, the cowboy allowed a smile to creep across his face, and he turned to the bartender. "Give this boy a drink on me," he said. Then he turned back to Nat. "There's a Texas outfit camped outside of town. Be there at six a.m. I hear they're hiring."

Nat was a brave young man, but on his way to the campsite that morning he was nervous. If he didn't play his cards right, his chance to be a cowboy could slip away.

When he reached the campsite, the trail boss was still having breakfast. He asked Nat to join him. Nat tried to look relaxed, but he felt like he'd swallowed a beehive. While the boss ate, he'd glance up at Nat to size him up. With all that talent back in Dodge City, he knew he'd be taking a chance, hiring a young boy with no experience. But so far he liked what he saw.

When he finished eating, he headed straight over to where they kept the wild horses. Nat and the other men followed. Turning to Nat, the trail boss asked, "So you want to be a cowboy. Can you ride a wild horse?"

Nat looked him straight in the eye. "Yes, sir!" he said. Actually, Nat hadn't been on anything wilder than those colts back in Tennessee, but, as I said, he had a heap of courage, and he was determined to become a cowboy.

The boss gave Nat one last look, then said to one of the other men. "Bring out Good Eye." Good Eye was bigger than all those Tennessee colts put together, and one of the wildest horses at the campsite. "If you can ride him, young man," the trail boss told Nat, "you got the job."

Nat knew he would have only one chance to prove he was cowboy material. The man that brought Good Eye over to Nat leaned over and whispered in Nat's ear, "He likes to go left, so ride him to the right." They had named him Good Eye because he was half-blind in one eye, and that is why he turned left.

It took two men to keep Good Eye still. The men eventually got a saddle on him and Nat's moment arrived. With all the courage he ever owned, he climbed up on Good Eye. When Nat was ready, the two cowboys let go, and Good Eye shot out into the sage like lightning let out of a bottle.

He bucked and jumped, threw his head up, and pitched left, just like the other cowboy said. "Ride him, young fella, ride him," the cowboys shouted. They all watched Nat do something none of them were able to do—stay on Good Eye. The horse tried every trick in the book to shake Nat like a bad habit. Finally, he gave up. Nat rode him over to the trail boss and dismounted.

"You're good, son, doggone good," the boss told him. "I haven't seen riding like that in a long time. What's your name, again?"

"Nat Love, sir," Nat answered.

"You got a job, young fella. We move out tonight." They shook hands and that was the beginning for Nat Love.

Nat learned all he could about the cattle business with this Texas outfit. He showed a strong natural talent for roping, riding, and shooting, and, as Nat's reputation spread, other job offers came his way. After three years, he decided to leave Texas for Arizona, where he had been offered a better position and more money with the Pete Gallinger company.

No one looking at Nat now, riding a big pretty chestnut-brown stallion, and decked out in his finest clothes and gear, would believe he had come from such humble beginnings.

Nat had gained a lot of experience by this time, but he soon came face to face with something that made him quake in his boots. It seems that Nat and some of the other cowboys working for Pete Gallinger had just gathered up a large herd of cattle down along the Rio Grande. Their job was to deliver the herd up north, hundreds of miles, from Mexico to Wyoming. That meant traveling through Texas Indian territory, Kansas, Nebraska, and the Shoshone Mountains—more Indian country.

The Indians didn't take kindly to cowboys driving all those cattle through their land without paying something in return. No, sir. This started many fights between the two groups. When cowboys didn't want to pay up, the Indians just took what they felt was fair. Luckily, Nat was usually able to work things out with them, maybe because of his color. The Indians generally respected the black cowboys because many of them were part Indian, and could speak their language.

Anyhow, Nat finally got his cattle to a place where the grass was short. That way, whoever had guard duty could see anything that moved out in the distance. One particular morning, as Nat stood watch, something peculiar happened.

"They're actin' strange this morning," Nat shouted to one of the other cowboys.

"Yeah, look at them moving around. Get back there!" shouted another cowboy to a steer.

Nat's horse suddenly reared up, and from a distance came the sound of roaring thunder.

The cattle were now moving in different directions. Nat and the other men were trying to contain fifteen hundred head of cattle.

"Nat, we can't hold them much longer," a cowboy shouted.

By now, the thundering sound was much louder, and every cowboy knew that certain sound buffalo made when they were on the run.

"Stampede, stampede," Nat hollered, circling the herd. The only way they could save the cattle was to turn the runaway buffalo in another direction. Nat's horse reared up again so every man could see him and, like a bullet shot from a Colt .45, all seventy-five men charged straight for the stampeding buffalo with guns blazing.

Riding and firing, they had hoped to swing the buffalo in another direction, but the buffalo weren't turning. As the cowboys got closer to the stampeding herd, Nat noticed that one of his men was having trouble controlling his horse.

Quickly, Nat swung his horse over to help, but right before his eyes, Nat's friend and his horse were cut down by the buffalo. By mid-morning, Nat and his men had recovered nearly all of their scattered cattle. They gathered what was left of their friend and gave him a proper funeral. Every cowboy knew his life could be snuffed out by an Indian's arrow, a gunfight, or an accident like a buffalo stampede. But no one counted on it happening to him.

The sun shone brightly in a clear, blue sky the morning of July 4th, 1876. Nat and his men had just delivered three thousand head of cattle to Deadwood City, South Dakota. The boys were feeling feisty and looking for some fun. Then word started circulating around town that some gamblers and mining men were putting together a contest.

"Can't nobody outride or outshoot Nat Love," one gambler said.

"You seem to be forgetting something, mister," a miner said. "You've got two hundred of the best cowboys in town today, including Stormy Jim and Powder Horn Bill."

"Two hundred dollars says White Head wins the shooting contest," said someone else.

When the trail bosses and gamblers finished talking, they decided that the first contest would combine roping, riding, and breaking a wild horse, all at the same time.

About then Nat walked over to the corral. "Can I get into this thing?" Nat asked.

"You're almost too late," one of the judges told him. "You'd better check in over there."

Nat quickly signed up for the first contest.

Next, the local sheriff talked to the assembled crowd. "You boys all know the rules. Wait for the gun, then go."

The man who could rope, saddle, bridle, and mount the mustang in the shortest time would be the winner. This was one contest that Nat was picked to win, hands down—his reputation with a rope and for breaking horses was legendary. So the trail bosses decided to play a little trick on Nat, to even the odds. A trail boss from Dodge City waited until Nat's number was called, then slipped into the corral.

"Is Glass Eye ready?" he asked the handler.

"You bet! Not even Nat Love can ride this killer," he said.

Nat had looked over most of the mustangs and was pretty sure he could handle all of them. "Number 35, Nat Love," called the sheriff.

When Nat heard his number, he hurried over to the stall to get ready. "I'm sorry to announce there's been a change. Nat Love will be riding Glass Eye today," the sheriff said, grinning.

Everybody thought Nat had met his match. He may have been a little worried himself, but it never showed, not one bit. Once Glass Eye was in place, Nat waited for the signal. When a Colt .45 pistol fired, Nat shot after the mustang like a wolverine after a weasel. It was something to see. He roped, saddled, bridled, and mounted that wild horse in nine minutes flat. That meant he was three minutes faster than the next closest contestant. Glass Eye didn't give Nat too much trouble at all.

Nat's next contest was the one that caused the most commotion—the one to decide who was the best shot in Deadwood City. The competition was fierce. The legendary cowboy Stormy Jim claimed to one and all that he was going to win, while Powder Bill and White Head swore that when they pulled a trigger, the bullet hit the mark on a dime. In that bunch were a few local fellows who fancied themselves pretty good with a rifle and a Colt .45. To settle the argument, the trail bosses set up targets, and marked off a distance of 250 yards for rifles, and 150 yards for the .45 pistols.

When all the shooting was over, only two men were standing to settle who was the best shot in the western territory—Stormy Jim and Nat Love. After both men reloaded and checked their guns, a trail boss flipped a silver dollar to see who would shoot first.

Jim won the flip. He stood at the line with his rifle, and fired ten shots. When he finished, eight bullets were in the bullseye. Then, at the signal, he drew his pistols and fired. Five of the bullets landed in the bullseye, and five fell outside. That wasn't bad shooting. Nat knew that he had some slick shooting to do if he wanted to win this contest.

It was Nat's turn. Everybody stopped what they were doing to see if he could live up to his reputation. Nat approached the line and studied the target. Then he picked up his rifle and did something that caught everybody by surprise. At the signal, Nat fired from the hip and placed all fourteen bullets neatly in the bullseye. Slowly, he laid his rifle on the ground, then he stood squarely in front of the next target. He waited for the signal, drew his Colt .45s, and placed all ten bullets in the bullseye. Stormy Jim couldn't believe it, but after he checked the targets, he had to go along with the judges.

From that day on, Nat Love became known as Deadwood Dick, Champion Roper and Best Shot of the western cattle country.

Nat used the name "Deadwood Dick" for some time after that. Everybody in the territory seemed to know about the shooting contest and how Stormy Jim couldn't believe his eyes when Nat neatly placed ten bullets in the bullseye of that target. When he left Deadwood City, Nat rode as proud and cocky as a champion rooster.

In Arizona, later that year, Nat and some of the other hands were collecting stray cattle that had been lost on the range. The men decided to separate so they could cover more ground and make sure nobody missed anything.

As the day wore on, Nat wandered off quite a few miles from the others. He was concentrating on finding lost cows or calves when, suddenly, his ears perked up like the back of a bobcat ready to strike. Even his horse knew that familiar sound. Spinning his stallion around in a full circle, Nat spotted the source of that familiar noise. Like an arrow shot from the tightly-strung bow of an Apache brave, Nat and his horse were off, running for their lives. The sound had been an Indian war whoop, and, from what Nat could see, the Indians had on their war paint and were riding straight at him. Quicker than a prairie dog scampering out of the way of a buffalo stampede, Nat pointed his stallion for Yellow Horse Canyon.

"Run, boy, run!" shouted Nat, giving his stallion full rein. The war party was gaining on him, so Nat turned to one of his tricks. Twisting his horse around, Nat galloped toward the Indians at full speed. He aimed his Colt .45 and squeezed the trigger. Well, Indians fell like apples from a shaken tree, but, still, those war yells got closer and closer. Now Nat's stallion ran for all he was worth. Nat's heart pounded harder with each thundering hoofbeat of the painted war ponies, and they seemed to be gaining on him with every stride. Bullets whizzed by Nat's head like hornets caught in an Easter bonnet. Yellow Horse Canyon got closer and closer, and Nat believed that if he could just make it there in one piece, he had a chance. Then something that felt like a hot branding iron tore through his leg into his horse, taking them both to the ground. Instinct told Nat that his horse was dead. Quickly using the stallion as a shield, Nat began to fight for his life.

As the light of day started to slip away, so did Nat's ammunition. He figured it would be just a matter of time before the Indians realized this, too. Sure enough, pretty soon Nat's worst nightmare came true. The Indians moved in and circled him. With the barrel of an empty rifle, Nat fought like a crazy man. As they tried desperately to overpower him, Indians fell, one at a time. Nat fought with nothing but his fists and an empty Colt .45. Blood flowed like a river from his leg and his fingers and nose were nearly cut off, but Nat struck back time and time again, like a wounded mountain lion, until the numbers of Indians proved too great.

When Nat came to his senses, he was in the Indian camp. "Where am I?" asked Nat, struggling because of the ropes that bound his hands and feet.

"You with Yellow Dog, now," said one of the Indians.

Nat tried to remember how long he'd been there. He wondered if the other men even knew he was missing, or where he was.

"We fix you good," said another Indian.

Nat looked at his leg and could see that it was almost healed. His fingers and nose seemed to be in the right places, too. He lay there, still puzzled about why they hadn't done him in.

"Why didn't you kill me?" asked Nat.

"You brave warrior, you fight like we fight. Strong fighter," an Indian replied.

As Nat looked around, he noticed that many of the

Indians had skin the same color as his. They were half-breeds, part Indian and part black.

"You like me," said another Indian, stretching out his forearm right alongside of Nat's face.

Considering that Nat was bound hand and foot, there wasn't much he could do, but his mind was working faster than the rapids of the Colorado River.

"Yeah, me brother, me hungry. Food, food," said Nat, smiling and grinning as he tried to gesture with his hands tied.

One of the Indians freed Nat's hands. Rubbing his wrists to get the circulation back, Nat kept motioning with his hands that he wanted food. Finally, the Indians understood, and they fed him all the buffalo meat he could eat.

Days passed, and all Nat's wounds healed perfectly. He had no idea what they had rubbed on his leg and fingers, but there were hardly any scars. Even Nat's nose had mended beautifully. By now, he was allowed to move around camp under the watchful eye of one of the braves.

As he walked around camp one evening, familiarizing himself with where the horses were kept, Nat noticed that all the braves were huddled around a fire, humming. He sensed that something important was about to happen. Suddenly, two of the braves got up and walked over to Nat. Grabbing him by the arms, they took him back to the circle. There, in the center of the inner circle, stood a brave, holding a small bowl of liquid containing two small bones that looked like needles.

"You brave warrior, fight like we fight. You brother. You with us, now," said the chief.

It didn't take Nat long to realize that he was being adopted into Yellow Dog's tribe. He didn't have much of a say in the matter, considering that both Indians held him like a stingy man holds a change purse full of pennies. Nat stayed quiet, as the Indian with the bowl of needles took one out and slowly pierced each of Nat's earlobes. Then strings made from tendons of a deer were placed through the holes and tied into knots. After more of the ointment that was used on his leg was applied to his ears, Nat was lead back to his tepee to rest.

The Indians believed Nat was one of them. They told him that those tiny bones used to pierce his ears came from a deer's leg, but they wouldn't show him how they made that powerful ointment. Nat picked up the Indians' sign language and could ask for whatever he wanted—anything but his freedom. Although Nat was an adopted brother, the Indians still watched him.

Finally, something happened that gave Nat the opportunity to escape. It seems that the chief had taken a strong liking to Nat. He went so far as to offer Nat four of his prettiest daughters to marry, as well as one hundred of his finest ponies.

"You choose. They are yours," said the chief in sign language. He pointed to his daughters.

Nat looked them over, knowing in his mind he was more interested in where the chief kept those fast ponies. "They are all too beautiful for one man to have, oh Great One, but in honor of your most gracious gift, I'd like to choose one pony," said Nat with his hands.

Few people knew where the chief kept his private ponies, so only his trusted braves rode out with Nat to select his gift. They took a very tricky route, but Nat marked every twist and turn in his mind. At last, riding into a small clearing, they came upon the most beautiful ponies Nat had ever seen. He dismounted and, while the others looked on, Nat checked out all the young horses until he spotted a

pretty chestnut-brown stallion that stood out among the rest. This horse had a proud neck and a high back and was just what Nat wanted. Nat could tell that he was a runner. He could also see that, just like Nat, he didn't mingle with the other horses much. If they got too close, he would break out, to stand alone. Nat knew when the time was right, he could easily find this beautiful horse again.

That night, Nat joined the Indians in dancing around a campfire. Everyone was in good spirits. Nat had pleased the chief in his selection of a pony and as far as they were concerned, he was one of them. Little did they know that Nat had already planned his getaway.

After all the Indians had danced themselves out, they went back to their tepees for a long night's rest. Nat was the last to stop dancing and return to his tepee. The Indians probably thought Nat was dead tired from all that dancing, but he was just playing possum.

Poking his head carefully out of the tepee, he looked around. No guards had been posted that night. As silent as a whisper, Nat crawled over 250 yards on his hands and knees. Then he continued on foot, remembering every twist and turn he saw that day, until he eventually made it to the ponies. Just as he had figured, there, all by himself, stood the stallion he wanted. Moonlight scattered a golden glow all over the horse's proud brown neck.

Careful not to stir up the other ponies, Nat crawled between their legs until he reached his stallion. Then Nat slipped a thin strap of buffalo skin in the horse's mouth to use as a bridle and, leaping onto his back, they headed for the open prairie.

"Come on, boy!" urged Nat, and that horse jumped into a gallop like he knew exactly what Nat wanted him to do.

Nat turned his stallion in the direction of Texas and never looked back.

When dawn broke in Yellow Dog's camp, the Indians realized that Nat was long gone. Twelve hours after he set out, Nat arrived safely back home in Texas. He had ridden more than one hundred miles on an unsaddled pony.

Nat kept that pony for five years, naming him "Yellow Dog Chief." The pony was too precious to waste herding cattle, so Nat rode him only on special occasions.

Even though Nat had left Yellow Dog's tribe, he gained a lot of respect for his Indian brothers. Nat remembered buffalo skin shields so tough that arrows couldn't pierce them; even rifle bullets might have bounced off them like hail falling on an adobe roof. Sometimes he'd laugh, thinking about how the chief never called him Nat, or Deadwood Dick. To the chief, Nat Love was Buffalo Papoose.

Nat was a special kind of cowboy. A free spirit, he stayed with an outfit only long enough to learn what he could. Then, like tumbleweed, he'd roll on to the next adventure. When old cowboys sit around campfires and tell tales of cattle drives up the Chisholm and Goodnight-Loving Trails, chances are, they'll mention Deadwood Dick. Of course, they'll be talking about Nat Love.

THE STORY OF
MARY FIELDS

Sundown, Sundown, come on back here boy. What are you chasing out there? Get on over here and settle down. I've got a tale for you I think you'll like. Boy, the West in those early days was as untamed as a mustang stallion. Some of the folks going out there were just as wild and full of vinegar as the land itself. Well, even a mustang can be tamed after a while, but it takes a mighty strong back and willful soul to do it. And Mary Fields was one of those folks—hardheaded and stubborn and full of snuff.

As near as I can remember, Mary Fields was born in Hickman County, Tennessee, around 1832. Like most African Americans born in this country at that time, Mary and her folks were slaves. They lived on a plantation owned by a white family, the Dunns.

"She's gonna be something one day, just see how she holds her head," Mary's mother used to say. Even as a baby girl, Mary showed early signs of being strong for her age, and had an independent streak the size of Texas.

By the time she was five years old, Mary could outrun and outfight any boy on the plantation. Early on, her daddy tried to teach her all about planting crops and doing chores, but Mary would as soon follow most of what her daddy said as cool off under a bale of cotton in the midday July sun. And when it came to planting cotton and doing other work around the plantation, Mary did them her way.

"I told you to pick the cotton this way, not like that," her mother would say. "Stop puttin' everything in the bag. Boss man gonna whup you. Now pay attention!"

Mary didn't seem to care. Picking cotton wasn't what she enjoyed anyway. Now riding horses—that was something. So when Mary's daddy explained how to plow the fields, Mary's ears perked right up. See, to plow the fields, work horses and mules had to be hitched up. Then Mary could mount the work horse, get the plowing done, and have herself some fun—all at the same time.

Mary grew into a big, strong woman on the Dunn's plantation. She learned to read and write, and when she got just about grown up, she picked up on smoking cigars and hanging around some pretty unsavory characters. Now, as a full grown woman, nobody could tell Mary what to do. She was her own boss, and bit by bit she took to running the plantation for the Dunns.

Earlier on, when she was just a youngster, Mary took to playing with Dolly, the Dunn's daughter. With not much for a little white girl to do on the plantation, and Mary doing more or less as she pleased, the two children played together a good deal of the time. Pretty soon, the two girls became good friends. When Mary found herself with some free time, the girls ran off and got into more trouble than a pack of raccoons.

Mary's mother took to brooding when she saw how close the two girls were getting. So one day she sat her daughter down and explained plantation life. "You just gonna have to start playing with your own kind. Them's white folks and white folks ain't like us. That's Master Dunn's little girl and he's got plans for her. As sure as cotton, she's leaving here and you can't go where she goes."

Mary didn't listen. She and Dolly had something special. But just like her mother said, as true as a hound's nose on the trail of a jack rabbit, Dolly grew up and moved away. Mary lost her best friend and it looked like the friendship was over for good.

Well, Mary lived and worked on the plantation for about 30 years. She really had no choice. And she wasn't the only one. Fact was that the South had tied itself to slavery the way one of Mary's plows was tied to those horses she loved so much. Most white folks down there couldn't imagine one without the other. But something as low down as slavery couldn't go on forever. The South and the North were working up a case of bad blood one against the other, and at last in 1861 these bad feelings broke out into the open. After four bloody years, the North won the Civil War, and Congress passed the Thirteenth Amendment, which made slavery illegal in these United States. This meant that Mary Fields was now a free woman.

A whole new way of living now lay before Mary. But for the time being, she decided to stay put with the Dunn family, doing odd jobs around what had become a much smaller plantation, now that all the slaves were gone. The Dunns treated her kindly, so when the family moved to Ohio, she went right along.

Ohio seemed a fine place, but Mary was never really happy there. A little piece of her life had ended when she had moved away from Tennessee, and it seemed to her that she was waiting for something new to begin. It was strange waiting for something you didn't know anything about. But Mary always had plenty of faith in herself. She was sure that sooner or later a sign would come to show her the way.

One day, when she was busy tidying up around the house, she got the sign she had been looking for. A letter, post-marked from out West, arrived with her name on it. Surprised, since she didn't think anybody kept tabs on her whereabouts, she opened it. In a lickety split, Mary's face lit up like a starry sky on a June night in Texas.

Her childhood friend Dolly was now a nun. *Sister Amadeus* is how she signed the letter, and she wanted Mary to join her at St. Peter's Mission, which was 17 miles from Cascade, Montana. After reading that letter, Mary dropped everything and made preparations to join her friend. Taking a teary-eyed leave of the Dunn family after spending 50 years with them, she headed straight West.

A lot of time had passed since Sister Amadeus and Mary ran like chickens around the Dunn plantation in Tennessee, so you can imagine the look on sister's face when she first laid eyes on Mary after all those years. Picture sister, staring up at a woman standing six feet tall, weighing two hundred pounds, wearing a man's pants and jacket, a six-shooter strapped low around her waist, and smoking a cigar to boot. The sight must have been enough to choke a mule. No matter, the two of them were pleased as punch to see each other, and Mary was ready for work.

The mission was old and in much need of repair. Workers were moving stones and fixing anything that needed fixing. Mary fit right in. She worked alongside the men, loading wagons with whatever materials they needed to get the job done. Many times, she picked up big boulders all by herself, or helped some of the men load timber. Mary enjoyed mingling and working with the men. She was as strong as most of them and had a leaning for hard liquor and rough talk.

It wasn't long before Mary became head honcho of the crew. From her childhood days, Mary always had her own way of doing things. But this didn't mean that the others were going to curl up and slink away. When she made herself boss, the men took to cussing and moaning. Many of them were white, and they didn't take too kindly to having a big black woman as head cowpuncher.

"Mind your own business, Black Mary," shouted one of the men.

"I'll mind *your* business, and if you don't like it, we can have a dust up right here in the street!" Mary said, with her cigar flapping in her mouth.

One day in July, it was so hot you could fry an egg in the palm of your hand. Mary was hauling stones for the mission. She had unloaded her wagon and, feeling sassy, started poking fun and meddling with the men. This one fellow was new, but that didn't bother Mary a tad. She treated him just like the rest.

"Okay Mister Sack O' Lard, get a move on it. We can pitch two stone shacks up here in the time you take for lunch."

A few men laughed. They were used to her by now. But this new fellow didn't think it was so funny.

"Since when does a black slave boss a white man?'' he asked.

"Ain't no slaves here, mister. Now I said, *move it.*"

Her voice filled with anger. Like I said, it was hot that day, and the stranger was tired and out of sorts. He walked up to Mary, swung, and knocked her square on her behind.

Everybody stopped what they were doing. They were watching like black birds in a cottonwood tree, their eyes on Mary, wondering what she would do. She was off the ground quicker than a hot knife through butter. Cigar still in her mouth, she dusted off her pants.

"Strap on your guns, mister, and meet me in the street,'' said Mary.

The workers couldn't believe their ears—a black woman putting a challenge to a white man for a gunfight. Nobody in those parts ever heard of such a thing. Course now, they didn't know Mary Fields.

The West in those days had a code, and this stranger knew it very well. If anybody, man, woman, or child, put out a challenge, you had to take it up or ride out of town. In this case, seeing how Mary was a black woman and he was a white man the alternative to fighting was more likely leaving the territory. The stranger strapped on his gun and moved slowly into the street. When he reached the center, Mary was there waiting for him.

At midday, Mary cast a shadow that seemed to block out one whole side of the street. Standing about twenty paces away from the ornery newcomer, she stared down on him, hard. Her face shined the color of a burnt prairie, and the smoke from her cigar curled around her head like a rattlesnake ready to strike. Quiet had fallen over the workers like a witch's spell. Mary stood her ground, waiting for the man to make his move. The fingers on the stranger's shooting hand twitched nervously, and he ground the heel of his boot into the dirt as he figured his shot.

Then, quicker than a squirrel can blink, the man went for his six-shooter. But Mary was faster. She fired three shots to his one, and the varmint keeled over into the dust, taking a last gander at the sun before knocking on heaven's door.

Mary, still chewing on her cigar, walked over to the mission grounds and started feeding the chickens.

"It was fair and square," she said, turning to the workers. "No man lays a hand on me." After that, no man ever dared to raise his hands again in Mary's face.

From that day on Mary had no problems with the workers, who were plenty eager to do whatever she wanted. But trouble did come from another quarter. It seems that the gunfight story spread throughout the territory and eventually got back to the bishop in charge of Sister Amadeus' region. He felt that Mary's reputation was causing more problems than the mission needed, and after 10 years of her devoted service he demanded that Sister Amadeus fire Mary.

You can imagine how low down Sister Amadeus felt that day when she got word from the bishop to let Mary go. She pleaded and begged, but he was stubborn as a can of lard.

"That black woman has become a nuisance. She has to go," he said.

Sister Amadeus knew she couldn't change the bishop's mind, but she also knew that she didn't want to part from her childhood friend. That night she thought and prayed about how to keep Mary at the mission, when, almost like a miracle, an idea came to her.

As luck would have it, a rumor had been circulating around town that the United States Mail service was opening a new route between Cascade, Montana, and St. Peter's Mission.

The new route was going to be tough. It followed a scrawny mountain trail that passed through badlands crawling with desperados and hostile Indians. Only the strongest and most experienced men even thought about taking the job. "That's it! Mary will get that job," Sister Amadeus thought, and history was in the making.

The next day, Mary got up early as usual, feeding the chickens and doing whatever else needed tending to around the mission.

"Mary can I speak to you a minute?" asked Sister Amadeus. "How would you like to help out the mission by handling some new duties?"

"You don't have to ask me. I'll do anything I can," Mary said.

Sister Amadeus explained to Mary about the mail delivery job. "It could be very dangerous. You don't have to take it if you don't want to."

Mary thought about it a minute. "If a man can do it, I can, and if a man can't do it, I can. Now who do I see about the job?"

Sister Amadeus told Mary that she had to be hired by the United States Mail depot manager. "He's a tough man, Mary. You have to really show him you can do the job," she said. Mary and the bishop knew that Sister Amadeus had already paved the way by going behind their backs and speaking to the depot manager. Now all Mary had to do was impress him, and she would have the job.

There were at least forty men standing around the depot that day looking to be hired. They all turned at once in the direction of thundering hooves and a cloud of dust.

Mary had arrived, wearing buckskin pants, a man's jacket,

and a Stetson hat. She jumped off her chestnut-brown stallion, and with a rifle in one hand and a cigar chomped between her teeth, walked through the crowd of men like a rooster parading around a barnyard full of hens.

"I'm here for the driver's job. Who's the boss of this here outfit?" Mary had a way of talking that sounded like an Army General leading his men into battle.

Out of the mail depot, came this stout little white fellow looking to see what all the commotion was about.

"I'm doing the hiring. Who wants to know?" he shouted.

Mary stepped right up and faced him square on. "I'm here for the mail driver's job. Where do I sign up?"

The depot manager looked at her carefully. "You're a woman. This is a job for a man, sorry." He tried to walk around Mary but she blocked the doorway.

"You hiring drivers, ain't ya? Well, I'm a driver and a darn good one," Mary said. "I can drive six teams of horses better than any man here."

The depot manager was getting just a little riled. He didn't expect a black woman to talk like this to him, especially in front of other white men. With his lips drawn tight across his teeth and his fists dug in on his hips, he said, "If you can drive six teams of horses better than any man here, you've got the job. But first you've got to hitch them up. They're over there." He pointed to the livery stable where they kept the horses.

Mary walked over to the livery stable and hitched those horses up so fast, it would have made you dizzy just watching. Faster than you can say giddy-up!, she had the horses' reins in one hand, a bullwhip in the other, and let out one loud "Move it!" With one crack of that whip, those horses took off like they'd been stung by a swarm of yellow jackets. Mary drove those horses around that yard in ten different directions, calling, "Move it! Move it!" Dust whirled over her head like a tornado. The crack of that bullwhip made it all sound like a Fourth of July celebration.

Mary brought the horses to a sudden stop right in front of the depot manager. Smiling at the crowd she asked, "Can any of you men do that?" No question, the depot manager was impressed, so much so that he hired her on the spot. And that's how Mary Fields became the second woman ever to carry the United States Mail. She was sixty years old when she got that job.

Delivering the mail in those days was not easy, no sir. More than once, Mary tangled with bandits and angry Indians. But once the Indians got used to seeing her, they became her friends. Soon, word spread throughout Indian territory, "Don't bother Black Mary." She was fast becoming a legend. Nothing, I mean nothing, kept Mary from delivering the mail on time. People out in that neck of the woods took to saying that if you rode past Mary's route, all you saw was a cloud of dust from her horses and smoke coming from that old cigar. If a bandit got too close, Mary would switch the reins to one hand, draw her six-shooter and fire, all the while going at full speed. Mary could shoot the tail off a jack rabbit at fifty paces. Maybe you can see how she earned her reputation as "Stagecoach Mary."

For eight years, Mary delivered mail from St. Peter's Mission to Cascade, Montana—always on time. Once, her horses gave out on her. It was one of those bad winters in Montana. The snow, nearly wagon-wheel high, slowed her horses down to a dead stop. Well, Mary just loaded the mail on her back, grabbed her rifle, and walked ten miles to the

depot. And would you believe it, she was just as punctual with the mail as usual.

Another time, Mary was racing back to the mission along old familiar trails, taking every shortcut she knew, and traveling as fast as her horses would run. She was in such a rush because Sister Amadeus had taken sick and needed special medicine. Also the mission's food supply was shorter than the eyelashes on a rattlesnake. Mary had loaded up the wagon with everything the folks at the mission needed, and the thought of Sister Amadeus laying there sick in bed drove her on without rest. Night was falling, and coming down over the top of a hill. She didn't see the dry gully below. When her wagon hit it, the sound was like thunder rolling across a dreary sky. Her freight was everywhere.

Quickly, Mary calmed her horses down. She could tell by the sun that she didn't have a lot of time before darkness would set in, and she knew what that meant—wolves and coyotes. Working faster and harder than ever before, she got almost all the freight back on the wagon, but by now darkness had crept in like a thief. There was a full moon that night, and Mary welcomed its light like an old friend. She knew how to take care of herself in the wilderness. Time ran out on her, otherwise she would build a fire to keep the wolves and coyotes away at night. See, they don't attack in daylight, just at night. With a finger married to the trigger of her rifle, she stayed up all night, firing into the darkness whenever the wolves got too close.

"Get back, all you rascals," Mary shouted, then fired her rifle in different directions into the darkness. Sure enough, it was a pack of hungry wolves. She could smell them and hear them yapping at her all night. "Come on over here if you want some hot lead for dinner," she yelled and fired a few more rounds.

When daylight came, Mary finished loading her wagon, and was off to the mission like a bullet shot from a Winchester rifle. Sister Amadeus, who was still very sick, started feeling better when she saw Mary rush in with the medicine and the much-needed food.

"I'm so glad you're back safely," she whispered.

"Don't you worry 'bout a thing. I'm here. Everything gonna be alright," said Mary. She nursed her best friend back to good health. Ten days later, Sister Amadeus was up and about like a young colt.

Eight years is a long time for a sixty-year-old woman to be hauling mail, even a woman like Mary. She finally gave up being a mail driver and, with the help of Sister Amadeus, opened a laundry business in Cascade, Montana.

Mary would do laundry on credit for cowboys who came through town on cattle drives. Sometimes, a few of them rode out of town, forgetting on purpose to pay her. Mary would let it slide by for a while, but one day she decided it was time to collect.

You'd thought by now Mary would have settled down, just a little. But one afternoon, Mary sat in the saloon having a friendly drink and enjoying good conversation with some of the boys, when she spotted a cowboy who owed her some money for laundry. As he got up and started out the door, Mary was right on him. She followed him a bit to make sure she had the right man.

"Hey you!" Mary shouted. The cowboy turned around. "You owe me for laundry. Now pay up!"'

He looked at her and laughed. "You got me mixed up with somebody else," he said, and turned to walk away.

"No I don't, cowboy," Mary said. She spun him around, and, with one punch, dropped him to the ground. She planted her foot deeply in his chest. ''Now pay me my money,'' she said.

The stunned cowboy reached into his pocket so fast that he pulled out all the money he had. Mary grabbed it, counted out what he owed her, threw the rest in his face, and walked away.

On her eighty-second birthday, Mary Fields was laid to rest. Her childhood friend, Sister Amadeus, had passed away a few years earlier, while opening up another mission in Alaska. The people of Cascade, Montana, had taken to Mary like a young boy to a stray pup. And it was in Cascade that she was buried, at the foot of a mountain trail that leads to a winding road heading for the old St. Peter's Mission. It was a road that Mary had traveled for many years, hauling freight and mail for a mission and a nun that she loved so well.

You know, Sundown, Mary Fields had the courage of two men. Legend has it that at night, when the winds blow down that mountain, you can hear the thundering hoofbeats of Mary's horses, her whip cracking in the night air, and a loud voice saying, "Move it."

CHEROKEE BILL

Sundown, when the Old West was growing and opportunities to start a new life were as plentiful as Texas cotton at harvest time, all kinds of people—some good, some not so good—came running. They came for every kind of reason you can think of. Some were looking for adventure; others were simply curious; many hoped to settle down on a bit of land they could call their own. A few wanted to escape from bad memories of things that had happened to them earlier in their life. Most of the people who came West looked to make their dreams come true by the sweat of their brow; a few saw their main chance in taking things that belonged to someone else. This last kind of person—the outlaws—remind me of someone I used to know.

Every man has a story explaining—or trying to explain—why he turned outlaw. Some folks were just downright mean or lazy. Others fell victim to the hatred and cruelty inflicted on them early in life. Now, this kind of person was not necessarily bad. He was just proud and willful, and his pride and will had been turned the wrong way by the treatment given him by his neighbors. One fellow in particular that I have in mind was a young man known as Cherokee Bill.

Crawford Goldsby, later known as Cherokee Bill, was born, around 1876, at Fort Conchos, Texas. His father, George Goldsby, was a sergeant in the Tenth Cavalry, and his mother, Ellen Beck, was a hard-working, God-fearing woman. Both parents were of mixed blood, part African and part Cherokee Indian. The family was upstanding and well respected.

Little Crawford's parents raised him good and strict at Fort Conchos. George Goldsby was a busy man who had little time for foolishness. Sergeant Goldsby's outfit, the Tenth Cavalry, was an all-black unit known as the Buffalo Soldiers. They were a crack regiment of the army and the proudest fighting black men this country has ever known. Yet, despite their brave service, the Buffalo Soldiers never received the respect they deserved from their white fellow soldiers or the white ranchers and townspeople they fought to protect.

Arguments flared up all the time between black and white troops. And the townspeople got into gun battles with the black soldiers—even though these soldiers risked their lives to protect the settlers from the attacks of hostile Indians. More than once the Tenth Cavalry rescued white soldiers pinned down by Indians. Unfortunately, the white soldiers rarely returned the favor. If the black soldiers got caught in a bind, they either had to fight until more men from the Tenth showed up or else fight their way out alone.

Little Crawford learned about the sting of racial prejudice early on. He listened intently as his father talked to his mother about the goings-on at Fort Conchos, and learned to tell by the sound of his father's voice when he got angry. Lately, that was happening more and more.

One night at the dinner table, Sergeant Goldsby couldn't hold in his anger any longer. "I'm sick of this business," he said bitterly to his wife. "Every one of my men could have been killed today rescuing those simple fools. I told the lieutenant they were riding into a trap, and he didn't believe me."

Ellen Goldsby tried to soothe her husband's feelings. "You did the best you could, George. There's nothin' more a man can do but that."

But her husband's anger was different and more intense that night. "They give us broken down horses and busted up rifles, and we're expected to save them every time they mess up. It's not right, Ellen. I just don't know how much more I can take."

As little Crawford watched his parents talk, he noticed a different look come over his mother's face as she listened to her husband. Something was happening, but Crawford couldn't figure out what it was.

Later that night, Crawford approached his father. "Are we going fishing tomorrow, papa?" he asked.

"I'll be riding out again in the morning, son. We'll go fishing as soon as I get back," his father promised.

Crawford enjoyed going fishing with his father. The boy would hear all about how his grandfather used to show his father the best way to hook a big one, and where to look for good fishing spots.

The morning after his father left, Crawford was awakened by voices in the next room. His mother was arguing with some man. Quietly, Crawford moved to the door of his room and peeked out.

"I said he ain't here and I haven't seen him since yesterday morning," his mother said.

"You must know where he is. He ain't been seen nor heard from all day. Now where is he hiding?" the white lieutenant shouted.

Crawford could sense something was about to happen. Breaking into the room, he pushed the lieutenant away from his mother.

"You leave us alone. My daddy will shoot you," said the seven-year-old boy.

"Oh he will, will he? And just where is your daddy?" asked the lieutenant.

"He surely doesn't know," said Crawford's mother.

"Well, if you see him before we do, tell him he's under arrest," said the lieutenant. "If he comes back here, he goes straight to jail."

"What did George do, lieutenant?" asked Mrs. Goldsby. "He's a good man and a good soldier."

"Your husband got into an argument with some white folks in town" said the lieutenant. "Instead of letting us take care of it, he and some other black soldiers took up arms against them. We can't have that kind of mess in Texas. How many times do we have to tell you people to stay in your place?"

"Did he kill anybody?" asked Crawford.

"Hush, now," said his mother. Standing tall and proud, she continued, "Whatever my husband did, I'm sure he was right."

When he heard that, the lieutenant turned and stared hard

at Mrs. Goldsby. "Like I said, y'all just don't know your place no how." As he walked out, he called over his shoulder, "If he comes back, George Goldsby's gonna hang by his black neck."

Crawford watched his mother try to hold back the tears. She didn't want to be weak, especially now, after what had just happened. But the tears came anyway, as she called out her husband's name more in fear for his safety than for her own. Hearing his mother's cry, Crawford's four-year-old brother, Clarence, woke up and wobbled like a wounded duck into the room. He missed all the action but, seeing his mother crying, he started to cry, too.

Crawford never did go fishing with his father again. The fact is, he never even saw his father after that. And it was some years before Crawford finally learned what had become of his daddy.

As Crawford grew older, the incident with the lieutenant never really left his mind. Meanwhile, his mother struggled to raise her two boys in the atmosphere of racial hatred that had torn her husband from his family. Life was difficult, and the Goldsbys moved around quite a bit while Ellen tried to scratch out a living for her family. She did the best she could with what she had.

When Crawford's mother saw that he was growing up fast, she realized that he needed to learn to read and write. Since she also thought it was time for him to learn about his Cherokee Indian background, she sent him off to a Cherokee Indian School.

The school was a big change for young Crawford. Never before had he been surrounded by Cherokee Indians. During his first day in class, he heard stories about his people that were told in Cherokee. He learned about how the Cherokees fought off the white soldiers and settlers who had tried to claim Cherokee land—land that had belonged to his ancestors. You could see the change starting up in Crawford. The more information he got about the greatness of his people, the taller he stood.

Before long, pride busted out all over him like cherry blossoms in the spring. By the time he left that school, Crawford Goldsby had changed his name to Cherokee Bill.

At the Carlisle School, in Pennsylvania, where Bill received a more formal education, everybody called him Cherokee Bill.

After two years at Carlisle, young Bill was nearly six feet tall. In spite of looking much older then he was, like most twelve-year-olds he missed his family and more familiar surroundings. Bill decided it was time to go home.

Returning home after three years, Bill had all the makings of a good-looking man. He rode up to Fort Conchos stylishly dressed, with his hair blowing in the wind. He remembered that the black soldiers were in another area, and rode around back. Faster than water dancing on a hot griddle, Bill dismounted and ran to the sergeant headquarters.

"Can I help you young man?" asked the black sergeant.

Bill, a little out of breath, said, "I'm looking for my mother, Ellen Goldsby."

The sergeant remembered that name. "You George Goldsby's boy?"

Bill was really taken by surprise. "You know my father?"

"I heard of him. He left the army some time ago. I ain't heard nothing about him since."

"My daddy was a sergeant like you, sir. I think he killed some white man for disrespecting him and his men," Bill said.

The old sergeant came over to Bill and put his arms around him. "I knew your father, boy, and as sure as I'm standing here, he was one of the bravest men I've ever seen. The army didn't do him justice, so he had to do what he thought was right. Judging from the way you seem to have turned out, I think he'd be real proud of you. Now, about your mother," continued the sergeant.

"You know where she is?" Bill asked. "And I had a little brother named Clarence, too."

The sergeant walked over to the files where the old records were kept and pulled out some forms. "Let's see," he said. "Yeah, your mama left here about three years ago. Looks like she and your brother went back to Kansas. She's living in Cherokee Indian Territory now."

Bill knew exactly where that was. He thanked the sergeant. Then quick as mercury, he was on his horse headed for Kansas.

Riding into Cherokee Indian Territory was not a pleasant experience for Bill. He saw his people all rounded up, living like bees in a honeycomb. He remembered the stories he'd heard in school about how his people had roamed all over this great land, fishing, hunting, and living at one with the land. Looking at his people now, relying on the United States government to feed them—a government that really didn't care if an Indian or a black man lived or died—made young Bill very angry.

"Do you know Ellen Goldsby?" he asked one of the first women he saw.

"She down there," said the woman, pointing to a small hut farther down the road.

Bill rode over to where she pointed. Excitement swelled in his lungs like wind filling the sails on a ship. When he knocked on the door, his fist nearly went through it.

"Who's making all that noise?" asked an angry male voice on the other side.

Once Bill heard that, his senses were snatched right back in his head. "Is a Mrs. Goldsby there? I'm her son, Crawford Goldsby," Bill said.

"Crawford, my baby," his mother shouted, as she rushed to get to him. She hugged and kissed the son she hadn't seen in over five years.

"Let me look at you." Ellen stood back, admiring her oldest child.

"My, my, you sure have grown up! Look at you!" She continued beaming with more pride than a farmer at harvest time.

"You gonna stand there all day, woman? I'm hungry," her new husband shouted. "Where's my food?"

"This is Crawford, my eldest," Bill's mother said, never taking her eyes off her son.

Her husband just looked at Bill.

"And son, this is Dunbar."

Bill looked into the eyes of his mother's new husband, "Glad to meet you sir," said Bill.

"So this is the one you keep making a fuss over," said Dunbar, finally. "I hope he turns out better than his worthless brother."

They all went inside and Bill's mother tried to catch up on all that happened in those five years. Since nobody paid him much attention, her husband decided to leave them alone.

"Where's Clarence?" asked Bill.

"He and Dunbar didn't get along," said his mother, "so he's staying with friends. But he's happy where he is, Crawford."

Bill didn't like that one bit. Point of fact, he didn't like anything about the reservation. It was sad for him to see his mother living the way she was, and it just increased the bitterness he felt toward everyone and everything, most especially toward white folks.

"You plan on staying here long?" his mother asked.

"No, I won't be here long. I'll be gone in the morning."

"But, Crawford, you just got here. Surely you'll want to rest for a few days."

"I don't need much rest these days," Bill said. "And another thing, Ma. I don't go by Crawford anymore. My name's Cherokee Bill."

His mother smiled. "You're a Cherokee, through and through. I'm proud of you, son. But remember, don't let no man push you around. You always stand up for your rights, you hear."

"Yes, Ma'am," Bill replied. "I aim to do just that."

He got up early that next morning, careful not to wake anybody. Bill saddled up, rode out of that little village, and never looked back. He knew he wanted something better, but what? That was a mighty powerful question on the mind of a twelve-year-old boy.

For the next eight years, Bill traveled throughout Indian Territory. He worked at many kinds of jobs, but the one he liked the most was working as a scout for the Cherokee, Creek, and Seminole Nations, learning more about his country and his people. The more Bill moved through Indian Territory, the more he saw white people gobble up land like a bunch of hungry chickens.

By 1894, Cherokee Bill had grown into a young man of eighteen. Standing six feet tall, with long black hair hanging to his shoulders, he was armed with a quick smile and loaded down with saddle bags full of charm. Bill was something to see. While working as a scout, he had mastered the craft of using a six-gun. Now, Bill could draw and fire faster than you could blink an eye.

Word had it that Cherokee Bill's life of crime started over a fist fight he got into one night in a dance hall. See, Bill was quite a ladies' man. According to the story, Bill was in a dance hall one night and a black man by the name of Jake Lewis had a girlfriend there who just couldn't keep her eyes off Bill. Since it was a dance, all the men had to check their guns at the door.

"Hey, pretty boy, keep your smiles to yourself, you hear!" shouted Jake to Bill.

"I believe it's the lady doing the smiling," Bill replied.

"Why don't we just step outside and we'll see who's mistaken, sonny," said Jake. He stood six-feet two-inches tall and rumbled around like a walking mountain, but Bill wasn't one to back down.

When the fight ended, Jake had beat the living daylights out of Bill. He lay there in the streets with blood running all down his brand new shirt. But what hurt most was his pride.

"I told you to keep your smiles to yourself, pretty boy!" Jake said, laughing as he walked back into the dance hall.

Bill got on his horse and rode out of town. Everybody figured he'd run off like a coyote with his tail caught between his legs, but they were dead wrong.

That same night, Bill came back, but this time he was wearing his six-gun. Everybody turned around when he kicked the dance hall door open.

"Jake Lewis, if you're a man, come on outside, right now!" said a bloody Cherokee Bill.

Jake looked at Bill and saw he was packing his six-iron. "You sure you wanna die, young boy," said Jake, smiling.

"Bring it out here," said Bill. As he backed out the door, his eyes never once left Jake Lewis. Once both men were outside, it was quiet for about a split second. After that, you could hear more gunfire than on the Fourth of July. When it got quiet again, Jake Lewis lay dead in the dirt, with two bullet holes in his chest. As soon as Jake hit the ground, Bill jumped on his horse and was out of there faster than a squirrel can blink.

Nobody had ever seen gunplay like that before. Bill had drawn his gun and, without taking his finger from the trigger, used the palm of his other hand to make a fanning motion over the hammer of the gun, causing bullets to fly everywhere. That's called "fanning," a style Bill himself invented, although many people tried to copy him later on nobody ever could do it better.

Now that he had committed his first crime, Bill was on the run. He looked for a place to hide from the sheriff's posse—a group of men assembled to ride after him. He'd got a good head start on the posse, but he needed to lay low for a while.

Riding into a small town, he headed straight for the saloon. It was there he met up with a rowdy bunch of boys called the Cook brothers. "So what you running from, boy?" asked one brother.

"What makes you think I'm running?" replied Bill.

"You got running written all on your face," said the other. "You kill somebody?"

Bill hadn't uttered another word before a man suddenly broke into the saloon. "It's Marshal Ben Jackson and his men, heading right this way," he said.

Quickly, the Cook brothers downed their drinks. As they hurried through the back door, one of them asked Bill, "Are you coming, boy?'' Without thinking, Bill grabbed his hat, and off he went.

Marshal Johnson and his men gave chase after Bill and the Cook brothers. The Cooks had a hideout high in the hills, and they got there just in time to set up and start returning gunfire. ''They ain't gonna never get us up here,'' one of the brothers said. ''What's your name, boy?''

Bill was too busy firing to hear the question. He aimed very carefully and squeezed the trigger. One of the marshal's men was killed instantly. ''Good shooting. You got one,'' said another brother. ''What did you say your name was?''

''Cherokee Bill,'' answered Bill.

Bill had killed his first lawman, and a bounty was on his head. After that, he and the Cook brothers went on a two-year robbing and killing rampage so fierce they became number one on the most wanted list. Reward money kept piling up higher and higher. Because Bill was so charming, he always had a place to hide. The ladies helped him many times to escape from the clutches of United States marshals and bounty hunters. He also knew the Cherokee, Creek, and Seminole Indian Territories like the back of his hand. So, while white marshals and bounty hunters had to fear for their lives, Bill could ride through Indian land untouched. For two years, Bill managed to avoid his pursuers until one day the chase ended.

Maggie Glass was one of Bill's girl friends at the time. The reward money for the capture of Cherokee Bill had been mounting up. By now it had jumped up to over $1,500! That was a lot of money back then. It seems that Miss Maggie decided she loved having that money more than she did Bill. One evening, she invited him over to meet one of her relatives. What Bill didn't know was that the man she invited over was no more kin to her than a raccoon is to a monkey. The man's name was Ike Rogers, and he was a United States marshal.

Bill showed up all decked out in his best clothes, wanting to make a favorable impression on Maggie's kinfolk. When he got there, he noticed that Maggie was the only one there. "Where's your cousin?" asked Bill.

"Oh, he'll be here shortly. He had a little business to attend to," Maggie replied. "Let me fix you a drink," she continued.

"That's okay, I'll wait till he gets here," Bill said. His instincts were working overtime. Maybe it was something in the way Maggie moved while she kept watching the window that made him uneasy.

"So what does he do?" asked Bill.

"I'm not sure exactly. I guess he'll explain that when he gets here," Maggie replied nervously.

Bill was sitting with his back to the door, when suddenly it opened, and there stood Ike Rogers, shotgun pointed right at Bill's head. "Don't move, Bill, or I'll blow you to kingdom come," shouted Ike. "Raise both hands over your head."

Bill did as he was told, as he stared coldly at Maggie. Sitting in the chair with his hands over his head, Bill rocked back on the hind legs a little.

"I said don't move," said Ike. Ike had the shotgun in one hand and his handcuffs in the other. As he stepped up to handcuff one of Bill's hands, quicker than the blink of an eye, Bill flipped back in the chair and knocked Ike down. Both men fought like wild dogs but Bill, being much younger, gained the advantage. He had wrestled Ike's six-shooter from his holster and was about to put a bullet in him when all of a sudden, Maggie knocked Bill out with a chunk of wood. When he came to, Bill was in a wagon, wearing handcuffs and leg irons, on his way to jail.

The trial of Cherokee Bill before Judge Isaac Parker in Fort Smith, Arkansas, was a major event. It seems as though Judge Parker also had a reputation—he was known as "Hanging" Judge Parker.

The courtroom was packed inside and out. Everybody wanted their last look at this dashing young outlaw named Cherokee Bill.

When he came before Judge Parker, Cherokee Bill was loaded down in chains. After Bill's lawyer finished making his case, Judge Parker calmly looked into Bill's face and sentenced him to hang by his neck until dead. The hanging was scheduled for sunrise the next morning.

"Ain't no jail made can hold Cherokee Bill," said one of the Cook brothers, who happened to be in the audience. Bill's mother was there, too. She pleaded with the judge to show mercy, but Judge Parker wouldn't hear of it. He was aware of Bill's escapes so he gave orders that no one was to speak to Bill in his cell.

The prisoner was helped down the steps to his cell underneath the courthouse with his mother following him.

"I'm sorry Ma'am, but you can't go no further. Judge's orders."

"He's my son. You gonna hang him in the morning. Can't you let a mother see her eldest boy before you take him away forever," she cried.

Now, normally, the guard would have stood his ground, but he looked at the twenty-year-old baby-faced Bill and, perhaps thinking about his own son, he weakened.

"You better make it quick. The judge will have my hide if he finds this out," he whispered. So he allowed Bill's mother a few moments alone with her son. And that mistake cost the guard his life.

As Bill's mother got close to the cell, she slipped him a gun. "Son, you ain't gonna die like they say. You ain't gonna hang like they hanged your father."

His mother's words hit Bill like a boulder dropped right on his chest. He never had found out what happened to his father. Growing up, he always figured his father had gotten away and was hiding out somewhere.

"They hanged papa?" Bill asked, his voice quivering with anger.

"You run, you hear me? They ain't gonna hang my boy. You get out of here," she said.

"Okay, let's go," the guard said finally, poking his head into the cell to see what was going on. By now Bill had hidden the gun in his shirt. "I'll lose my job for sure if they hear about this," he continued.

Those were the last words that came from his mouth before Bill opened fire, killing him right away. Quickly, Bill got the key and unlocked his cell.

"What's going on down there?" asked another guard, coming down the steps. He turned a corner, only to meet another bullet from Bill's gun.

Now Bill was out onto the street, running for a free horse. Gunfire from the other guards rained down on him like a Texas hail storm, but they all missed their mark. Bill jumped on the back of the first hitched horse he passed, and with guns blazing in every direction, he headed for the far end of town. Suddenly, like a tree struck by lightning, his horse hit the ground. One of the guards had shot Bill's horse out from under him. With Winchester rifles staring him in the face from every direction, Bill threw down his gun. It was all over. Back to jail he went, this time to stay.

Bill was already up and carrying on like he was going to a picnic as the first light of dawn crept through the cell window. "Let's go," said the guards. They walked him up from the cell into a courtyard full of people. About twenty-five feet ahead stood the gallows. Judge Parker had allowed Bill's mother to walk with her son one last time. Since he was handcuffed, there was no chance of her slipping him anything this time.

"Looks like something's gonna happen," said Bill, as he looked out over a crowd of one hundred or more people. His mother watched her eldest son, whistling, and acting like he couldn't wait to get it over with, march up the steps to his death. She didn't say a word, just stood there as the hangman placed a rope around her son's neck.

"Have you got anything you'd like to say?" Judge Parker asked Bill.

"I didn't come to make a speech. I came here to die," said Bill. That was all he said. On March 17, 1896, Cherokee Bill—that is, Crawford Goldsby—was hanged until dead.

They say that Bill's younger brother Clarence caught up with Ike Rogers and shot him to death. Nobody knows for sure what happened to Clarence after that. Some say that he was never captured. As for Maggie Glass, I don't know whether or not she ever did get that reward money. Since Ike was killed shortly after Bill's hanging, she just might not have collected a penny. As I said before, Sundown, life's funny. Given a different deal of the cards, Cherokee Bill might have turned out better. I guess that's something we'll never know.

BLACK UNITED
STATES MARSHAL,
WILLIE KENNARD

*S*undown, *not much was known
about Willie Kennard before he rode into the small mining town of
Yankee Hill, Colorado, around 1874. For a time, Willie had been a
Buffalo Soldier, and he made the rank of sergeant before his
discharge. As a Buffalo Soldier, Willie fought with some of the
bravest men who ever wore a uniform.*

"Where you headed, Willie, now that your tour of duty
is over?" a white lieutenant asked him one day.

"I don't know right off, sir. I guess I'll go where I can
find work."

"You're a fine soldier, a credit to the Ninth Cavalry. I
wish you the best."

Willie had served well as a Buffalo Soldier and took pride in whatever he did. No matter how dangerous the mission, you could count on Willie Kennard to be there. He stood over six feet tall and was a quiet man—not one for much conversation. But when he drew his gun, everything stopped, including anyone who went up against him.

"Stay in touch," said one of the older Buffalo Soldiers, as Willie mounted his horse, and headed out of Kansas for Colorado.

Willie had read an ad in the *Rocky Mountain News* about a small town in Colorado that was looking for a marshal. With his experience as a soldier, Willie figured he might as well apply for the job.

"I'm sick and tired of all these killings," said Mr. Owens, the Yankee Hill town barber. "This is the twelfth man shot down in the streets in a week, and you sit there doing nothing."

The mayor squirmed in his chair. "Now just one minute, Owens. We've gone through six marshals in two weeks. It ain't my fault we can't keep nobody."

"You're the mayor, and if you want to be elected come November, you better do something quick," said Mr. Owens.

"Do what? I can't go up against Barney Casewit. He's crazy," said the mayor.

"No, *we* were crazy to elect you mayor," Owens said. "A town meeting is coming up, and I think the decent people of Yankee Hill might want a new mayor." The mayor slammed the door on his way out. His shave was about as rough as life was becoming in Yankee Hill.

Like a lot of little mining towns, Yankee Hill had sprung up like a bad sneeze. People came from everywhere, still hungry for gold. Yankee Hill had its hands full. It seemed like gunfights were the only way to settle any argument, and one man with a powerful nose for trouble and for killing people was Barney Casewit. A big white boy in his late twenties, Barney had ridden into Yankee Hill with some of his boys, and saw an opportunity to take over the town. If he wanted something, he just took it, and if it was yours, he'd kill you first and take it afterward. He and his men did as they pleased because nobody was brave enough to stand up to them.

One day, in the saloon, the mayor made an appeal to Barney. "Mr. Casewit, we just have to stop all these killings. The people are starting to complain, and I'm getting a bad name."

"Complain? Complain about what?" said Barney. "They all know I run this town, not you. If they got something to complain about, send them to me."

"Sure, Barney, but maybe you could slow things down a little, until the townfolks relax," the mayor pleaded.

Barney just laughed and shoved him aside. "I'll do as I please, and you know it. Now get out of here. I'm tired of listening to you."

That was about the extent of the mayor's conversation with Barney. He had enough sense to know that if he didn't leave at that moment, he might be carried out in a pine box.

Relying both on the map and on his keen sense of direction, Willie Kennard knew he was just a few hours from Yankee Hill. He had decided to stay at a boarding house and ride into town fresh the next morning. Now, staring up at the ceiling from his bed, Willie thought about his days and nights as a Buffalo Soldier. He had made quite a few friends and left a lot of dead enemies behind.

Willie picked up the newspaper and read the ad one more time. "...no experience necessary," it said. He thought that was a little unusual, considering that a marshall needed know-how to handle his job. After a while, Willie reached over and turned out the light. Once again, his mind reflected on where he had come from and where he was going, until he fell sound asleep.

Willie was up bright and early the next morning. He'd just finished shaving and was checking his face in the mirror. He felt confident that he looked as sturdy and dependable as a brick jailhouse. Whoever was doing the hiring was sure to cotton to him. It had never dawned on Willie before, but for a brief moment, he wondered if any black people lived in Yankee Hill. No matter. If he got the job, he'd be everybody's marshal. Then Willie wondered if anybody else had applied for the job. Well, his questions would soon be answered.

Willie hadn't been sure what to expect, but what he saw was a true surprise. Yankee Hill was a mining town, all right. Everywhere you looked, there were crowds of people in the streets. Willie counted more saloons than general stores and—yes—he heard gunfire. There was too much commotion going on for anybody to notice Willie Kennard as he slow-trotted his beautiful black stallion right through the middle of town, tipping his hat to startled white ladies as he searched for the mayor's office.

When he found what he was looking for, Willie rode over and dismounted. The mayor and Mr. Owens were having another argument.

"This is the last straw. If you can't find someone to protect the upstanding people of this town, you'd better pack up and leave," yelled Mr. Owens.

"You want the job as mayor, you got it. I resign!" shouted the mayor.

They were so busy chewing each other out that at first they didn't see Willie. Finally, the mayor noticed this tall black man standing there.

"What are you staring at, boy?" he said.

"I'm putting in for the marshal job," said Willie with an even voice.

The mayor looked first at Mr. Owens, then back at Willie. "You what?" asked the mayor, as if he couldn't believe his ears. A black man riding into an all-white mining town wanting to be their marshal—it didn't make sense to him.

"This paper said you were hiring, so I'm here to put in for the job," said Willie.

"I know what the paper says," answered the mayor. "*I* placed the ad. We ain't hiring no . . ." Suddenly, Mr. Owens pulled the mayor to the side and whispered something to him. A smile flashed across the mayor's face. "Well now, if you really want to be the marshal of our fine little town, you got to prove you can do the job," said the mayor, rubbing his hands together like he was trying to start a fire.

"I've got experience as a soldier, and I also know how to keep good records," Willie announced proudly.

"That's fine, but we're not concerned with your record-keeping. We've got another task for you. But before we swear you in," said the mayor, reaching into his pocket and fishing out a marshal's badge, "Put this on. There. Now you're a temporary marshal. If you can carry out your first assignment, you've got a full-time position here in Yankee Hill," said the mayor, trying to hold back from laughing.

Those two may have thought they were playing a joke on Willie Kennard, but when he put that badge on, in his mind, he *was* the marshal, and doing the job well was all that mattered. The mayor could see something in Willie's face he hadn't seen in the faces of the others who had applied for the job. Willie carried himself like he was important, like he was somebody. What started out to be a joke didn't look too funny anymore, and the mayor started to get cold feet, thinking he was sending a good man to his death.

"Listen, you don't have to take this job. Maybe this one's not for you," said the mayor in a more civil tone than he had used before.

"You haven't told me what I have to do yet," said Willie.

"We've got a big problem. His name is Barney Casewit. Barney has killed every lawman who's tried to arrest him, and I'm sure you'll be next."

"I said I wanted the job. Where is Mr. Casewit?" Willie asked.

The Mayor pointed to a saloon where he knew Barney spent a good deal of time.

"I'll be back directly," said Willie, walking in the direction of Barney Casewit.

The sun was high that day. Willie's badge reflected so much sunlight that you couldn't see his face.

"Now would you look at this, Barney? Come over here and see what new lamb these townfolks have brought for you to slaughter," said one of Barney's men.

As Willie walked over to the saloon, what was usually a busy street overflowing with people looked like a ghost town. Even though he couldn't see anyone, Willie knew all their eyes were on him. Meanwhile, Barney peered over the

saloon door and watched Willie getting closer and closer. Then he saw Willie stop.

"Mr. Casewit, come out. Drop your gunbelt and follow me," Willie commanded with so much authority that even Barney was surprised. Turning to his men in the saloon, Barney grinned like a sly fox. "I'm gonna enjoy this one most of all," he said as he kicked open the saloon door.

"You overstepping your manners, ain't you?" shouted Barney.

Willie was standing about thirty feet from Barney. He kept his eyes on Barney every second. "This is the last time I say it. Drop your gunbelt and come with me!"

Barney was wild with rage. No man ever raised his voice to him and lived to talk about it, and here this black man was standing there, ordering him to drop his gunbelt and actually follow him to jail. Anger swelled up inside him like air in a bullfrog's belly.

"You want this gun, boy, you crawl over here and get it!" snarled Barney.

Some of the townspeople, taking it all in at a safe distance, never heard anybody talk to Barney that way before. Watching as Willie ordered Barney to drop his gun gave them a new sense of pride.

It was so quiet that for a split-second you could hear the air crackling. Then it happened. Quicker than the twitch of a jack rabbit's nose, Willie drew his gun and fired. His bullet went straight through the bullet chamber of Barney's gun, ripping it apart in his hand. Nobody in Yankee Hill ever saw anything like it. When Barney's boys saw it, they filed out of the back door of that saloon like roaches running from the light. Barney stood there holding his hand and shaking like a wet puppy. After that, Willie walked up to Barney and led him off to jail without a peep. Shortly after his arrest, Barney Casewit was tried by a jury, found guilty, and hanged by the neck until he was dead.

Sundown, you can believe that the townspeople gave Willie all the respect fitting a United States marshal. His reputation with a gun became legendary throughout Colorado. I never did hear what happened to the mayor of Yankee Hill. I wouldn't be surprised if the townspeople elected him governor or something. As for Willie Kennard, he stayed on as marshal of Yankee Hill for two more years before he finally moved on.

As little is known about the end of Willie's life as the beginning. I wouldn't be surprised if he just kept heading west until he hit California. He probably served as a lawman at a few other towns along the way. You just don't find many men like Willie. He was the best there was.

BILL PICKETT, "THE DUSTY DEMON"

*N*obody *knows better than you and me, Sundown, about the special bond a man and his best friend can feel. But Bill Pickett's best friend was a horse, not a dog. Together, Bill and Spradly claimed their own special spot in rodeo history.*

Bill came into the world around 1860, shouting and screaming. His family, like lots of other black families, was already in Texas even though the Civil War was still going on. Although most black people were still forced to work as slaves, some were arriving in places like Kansas, Colorado, and Texas, looking for a better way of life. Texas is where Bill's folks settled and that's where he was born.

Growing up in a place where the land stretched farther than the eye could see was perfect for a boy like Bill. His mother would watch him play with the cows and horses on their little piece of land and think about how unafraid her son was of those big animals.

"Bill, you be careful foolin' around with them horses," she'd say.

Bill would listen to his mother but, deep down, he knew the horses and cows were his friends. When his mother took him into town, he would run off to watch some of the cowboys "horse around." When they gathered at the far end of town to race their horses for money, Bill was right there watching.

There's something about Texas that makes a boy grow up fast. By the time he was thirteen, Bill had already worked for quite a few ranches in the area. He especially liked working with the wild horses and longhorn steers. Bill had a mighty peculiar power over animals. He could look a stallion in the eye, talk real low to him, and make that horse do anything he wanted. There aren't many who have this gift, no sirree.

Well, Bill grew up faster than a young colt on fresh grass. He was one of thirteen children, and it was pretty crowded around the home front. At fifteen, Bill's yearning to see the other side of the mountain flared up like a forest fire, and he knew the time had come for him to move out and earn his keep. Cowboys talked a good deal about a place called Oklahoma, so Bill just saddled up one day, and was Oklahoma bound.

After a long, hard day of riding, Bill spent a night sleeping on the ground. That next morning, he rode into a small town on the outskirts of Oklahoma, looking for work. He trotted over to the livery stable where some cowboys were breaking wild mustangs. Charlie, the blacksmith, was shoe-

ing a horse when Bill walked up to him.

"Where can a man get a job around here?" Bill asked.

Without looking up, Charlie bellowed, "What can you do, boy?"

Bill had to step back from a voice that sounded like a herd of runaway buffalo. Then, pulling himself together and speaking in as manly a tone as he could, he said, "I'm good with horses."

Finally, Charlie looked up and said, "See that pinto over there? Bring him to me."

Bill spotted the horse and overheard some cowboys laughing. "Can't nobody get within ten feet of that pinto," one cowboy shouted.

An older fellow pulled young Bill to the side, warning him, "Careful, boy, that horse's got a whole lot of wild left in him. Tell Charlie to pick another horse."

But Bill looked at Charlie and winked. Next, he climbed over the corral fence, shooing away the other horses until it was just him and that pinto. Nobody could hear what Bill said because he spoke real soft and low. The pinto reared up, then came right at him, hooves pounding in the dirt. Bill stood his ground and kept on talking, moving closer and closer until he had his hand on the pinto's nose. Still whispering and stroking its neck, Bill grabbed a handful of mane and swung up on the horse's back. The pinto reared up and whinnied one time and that was it. Bill trotted him right over to Charlie, as smooth as churned butter.

All the time this was going on, a white man standing a few feet away saw everything. The man's name was Zack Miller. Zack and his brother owned the 101 Ranch. He hired only the best cowboys in the territory. Zack walked over and shook Bill's hand.

"I liked what you did with that stallion. Mighty fine

work, son. I'm Zack Miller. I own the 101."

"I'm Bill Pickett, and I'm looking for work," said Bill.

Zack had been around, and he knew talent when he saw it. Bill definitely had something. "I'm always looking for good people. Where you staying?" Zack asked.

"Right where I stand," said Bill. "I just rode in today."

"Then saddle up," Zack told him. "We could use a man like you at the 101." That ride to the 101 changed Bill's life forever.

When they rode up to the 101, Bill was mightily impressed. There were over 100,000 acres, all in the hands of two brothers. Bill could hardly believe that two people owned so much land. And there he was, with a brand new job that would have him riding all over the property like he owned it.

Zack Miller treated Bill like his natural son. He took Bill under his wing and taught him the business. Bill was a fast learner. Quicker than lightning, he picked up every trick the other cowboys threw out as well. Bronco-busting and roping calves came as naturally to Bill as kick in a mule. He could handle a branding iron like it grew out of his hand. Shooting was as easy as spitting. In fact, the best pistol and rifle shots around would pass up the opportunity to bet against Bill. But it was his skill with horses and roping calves that really made Bill special.

Just a young man in his prime, Bill was becoming famous. Word had it that Bill could do things with a rope that a magician would envy. If a rodeo stunt wasn't dangerous or didn't challenge his spirit, he wouldn't do it. Zack Miller had two hundred of the best cowboys in Oklahoma, and Bill Pickett was number one. He paid particular attention not to let the others get too close to that number.

One evening, a cowboy approached Bill. "What's on your

mind, Bill? You been sitting on this fence all evening."

"I just been thinking, that's all," replied Bill.

"Well, I bet a week's pay, it's about your next trick," the cowboy said, as he walked away.

The following week, Bill and a few other cowboys from the 101 drove a herd of longhorn steers into Texas to load on stock cars headed east. It had been a long ride, and many of the men couldn't wait to quench their thirst at the local saloon. But first, they had to get these steers safely on board the stock cars.

Things were going pretty well when all of a sudden some cowboy yelled, "He's loose! He's loose!"

Bill spun his horse around faster than the blink of an eye and charged after the runaway steer. What he did next would make a hungry mountain lion back off his prey. Galloping full speed, he caught up with the steer, jumped off his horse onto the steer's horns, and twisting that renegade's head around, bit him on his top lip. That animal hit the ground like a sack of rocks. From that day on, Bill Pickett had a new trick he called "bulldogging."

Bulldogging got its name from the technique that some Texas cowboys used in training bulldogs to free cattle from heavy underbrush. Once a steer was free, the bulldog would jump up and bite the animal in a tender spot under the nose, and bring him down. Bill Pickett was the first cowboy to try on this way of steer wrestling.

Zack Miller realized that Bill was becoming famous. Cowboys from all over the territory were talking about how Bill Pickett could ride and jump off his horse and wrestle a full-grown steer to the ground. Some of the other cowboys mustered up enough courage to try Bill's stunt, and it wasn't long before bulldogging became a favorite cowboy pastime. Since Zack had two hundred of the best-trained men as well as Bill Pickett, he decided to take his ranchhands all around the country to show everybody what they could do.

One day, back on the ranch after a long rodeo tour, Zack spied Bill all alone out on the veranda of his bunkhouse. "What are you thinking about now, Bill?" Zack asked him.

"I'm thinking I need me a special kind of horse, and I haven't found him yet," said Bill.

Zack took Bill over to his stables, where he kept his best horses. "Pick whichever you want."

Bill went over those animals like a dandy fixing his hair with a fine-tooth comb. He stared them in the eyes, opened their mouths, did absolutely everything looking for that special connection that only he and the right horse could make. Disappointed, he started to leave, when he noticed a sickly, dark-brown young stallion with a white diamond patch on his forehead, laying down in his stall. Bill would have walked right by if that stallion hadn't raised his head, looked Bill square in the face, and whinnied. That was the connection Bill was looking for.

"You're the one," Bill said.

"What's going on in there?" Zack shouted. He came around back of the stables to see what was happening.

"I found my horse. He's the one," said Bill.

"You can't mean Spradly. He's sicker than a cowboy on a Sunday morning. I'd planned to put him down," Zack replied.

Bill looked into Spradly's eyes. "He's gonna be just fine. You'll see. You said I could have any one I wanted. I want this one."

Zack looked at both of them and shook his head. "A deal's, a deal. He's yours."

As I said before, Bill had something special with animals. He and Spradly were together day and night. Bill worked with the horse and talked to him like he was human. In about a month, you could see the change in that animal. He just got stronger and stronger. And whatever Bill wanted Spradly to do, Spradly would do. You might say he was a true cowboy's horse. Understand, a cowboy has to depend on his horse like he depends on his gun. They have to be of the same mind. For example, if the cowboy thinks right but the horse goes left, the cowboy can be thrown from his saddle. One look at Bill and Spradly and there was no question, those two were sharing a saddle.

Spradly was so well-trained, he could corner a calf all by himself. When those two were bulldogging a steer, you could swear Spradly was talking to Bill about the best way to come up on him. Those two were something to watch.

The 101 Wild West Show drew crowds of young cowboys and girls everywhere they went—from Texas to Oklahoma to Kansas. Zack even carried his show east to Chicago and New York City, wherever he could draw the biggest crowd. Everybody wanted to see the "Dusty Demon," Bill Pickett. Thrilling the crowds and doing something different was Bill's way, and he never failed to please.

One evening, the men were gathering their things together for a show they were doing in Mexico, when Bill rode up on Spradly. He overheard a few fellows talking.

"He put five thousand dollars cold cash on Bill," one said.

"If Bill does that, then he's a damn fool," said another.

About that time, Zack walked over to Bill and pulled him aside. "I want to talk to you a minute. I guess you overheard them talking about a bet I placed on you. You don't have to do it, but I'll be danged if I'll let any man say Bill Pickett is short on heart."

"What was the bet?" Bill asked.

"You know we go into Mexico tomorrow? Well, I bet a fella with a lot of money that you would bulldog a bull named Little Bean."

Bill stood there, rubbed his neck, and flashed Zack a smile as wide as the state of Texas. "Then you're sure to win."

Every man riding with the show heard that Bill had agreed to take the bet.

"Is he crazy? Who does he think he is?" a cowboy asked.

"Can't no man bulldog Little Bean. He's a killer," another one replied, as they rode into Mexico—Bill Pickett and the two hundred men of the 101 Wild West Rodeo Show.

Word traveled all over Mexico that Bill Pickett would bulldog Little Bean. The crowd that day was as eager to see the show as a hungry bear with a honey pot. Little Bean had killed two or three matadors in a bullfight already, and everybody thought Bill Pickett was next.

Once the rodeo got underway, you could feel something different in the air. Each cowboy was taking more and more chances than ever before. Some stayed on wild bucking bulls longer than necessary. Others picked out mustangs they knew were especially dangerous. That day, each cowboy felt like showing off. Nobody wanted to look less than brave, not in front of twenty-five thousand people who were really there to see Bill Pickett.

Finally, the moment arrived. All roping and bronco-busting acts were over and the arena was empty. Bill and Spradly were in the back, and Bill was talking to Spradly like a father to his son. Bill looked cooler than a satisfied rooster. You have to wonder how he must have felt inside. I'll bet his heart beat faster than an Indian war drum.

" . . . and now señors and señoritas," said the ringmaster, from way up in the stands.

Suddenly, there was a noise like boulders falling down a mountain. Women in the crowd screamed. Little Bean had broken loose and was in the arena.

Those Mexican horns started playing and quiet fell over the crowd like a hungry wolf sneaking up on his prey. Little Bean strutted around that arena, sweat lathered up all over his body and white foam dripping from his mouth. He twisted his head right and left like he was looking for Bill. Then, with his head down, he pawed the dirt and waited.

Lightning couldn't have come out of a thundercloud faster than Bill and Spradly shot out of the back entrance of that arena, headed straight for Little Bean. Bill's hat was pushed back on his head from the speed of Spradly, who galloped with more courage than a mustang stallion. Before Little Bean knew what had happened, Bill jumped off Spradly onto the horns of that bull, twisting his head up, sinking his teeth into the bull's top lip, and dragging him to the ground.

Twenty-five thousand people went crazy. They threw hats, flowers, anything they could get their hands on, to show Bill Pickett their admiration. Bill didn't take too many bows. Actually, he got out of that arena pretty quick. But that day, at a Mexican rodeo, everybody saw one of the West's most famous cowboys do something nobody had ever done before—bulldog a raging bull.

Eventually, Bill left the 101 Wild West Show. He was getting older and he'd made enough money to support his parents and brothers and sisters. He was proud of his record as the number-one cowboy in the country, and now it was time to sit back and take life easy.

Well, being away from the rodeo life for a spell, your skills get a little rusty. But I guess once you're a cowboy, it's in your blood forever.

After he left the 101 Show, Bill went on to Hollywood to make a few silent movies and show off his talent as the number-one cowboy in the country. He was so famous that everybody wanted to meet him and ask questions about his skills. A couple of white cowboys by the names of Will Rogers and Tom Mix got to know Bill pretty well back then. Both of these fellows learned a lot from Bill Pickett while working on the 101 Ranch. They later went on to Hollywood and became big movie stars, even bigger than Bill. Funny how that happened. Bill was the biggest star of all the rodeos. Tom Mix and Will Rogers used to ride out and get Bill's horse after he finished bulldogging. Yet when Bill went to Hollywood, California, he only made three movies. White cowboys were just easier for the American public to accept.

Later on, in 1932, when he had pretty much set himself out to pasture, Bill went out on foot, looking for a stallion he'd had his eyes on for some time. One day, when he finally got close enough to put a lasso around the stallion's neck, that powerful horse turned on Bill and charged. Then he reared up and smashed Bill in the head with his right hoof. A few days later, one of this country's most courageous cowboys was dead. His good companion, Spradly, had died of old age, just a few days before. I can tell you, Bill Pickett will never be forgotten. He made his mark on the face of the Old West forever.

Well, as the Old Cowboy said these last words, a few tears, bright and sparkly as Missouri River quartz, began to well up in his eyes. Sundown noticed that his master had misted up some, and so he commenced to howl at the moon.

"Ah, now don't you go and get sentimental on me now," the Old Cowboy said, straightening himself up. *"Ain't no use crying over days gone by. Besides all those folks—good and bad—lived life to the fullest."*

It was getting mighty late now. The moon was on its way down. Sundown shuffled around the porch and yawned.

"Well, alright then," the Old Cowboy said. *"I reckon we ought to call it a night."*

And then the two of them, man and beast, best friends to the end, disappeared inside the door of their cabin. But they won't be gone long. As long as there is a good story that needs to be told about the West, the Old Cowboy and Sundown will be around to tell it.

BIBLIOGRAPHY

Bonner, T.D. *The Life and Adventures of James P. Beckwourth.* New York: Arno Press, 1969.

Durham, Phillip, and Jones, Everett L. *The Adventures of the Negro Cowboys.* New York: Dodd, Mead & Co., 1965.

Goode, Kenneth G. *California's Black Pioneers.* Santa Barbara, CA: McNally & Loftin, 1974.

Katz, William Loren. *Eyewitness: The Negro in American History.* Belmont, CA: David S. Lake Publishers, 1974.

Katz, William Loren. *The Black West.* Seattle, WA: Open Hand Publishing Inc., 1987.

Katz, William Loren. *Black Indians: A Hidden Heritage.* New York: Macmillan, 1986.

Lee, Irvin. *Negro Medal of Honor.* New York: Dodd, Mead & Co., 1967.

Stewart, Paul W., and Ponce, Wallace Yvonne. *Black Cowboys.* Broomfield, Col.: Phillips Publishing, 1986.